wearwithall
KNITS FOR YOUR LIFE

Mary Lou Egan

Theresa Gaffey

Scott Rohr

Shelly Sheehan

Sarah K. Walker

photography by

Gale Zucker

Printed by Printing Enterprises, Inc., New Brighton, Minnesota

Copyright © 2012 840 Books

ISBN 978-0-9851621-0-8

Designer: Sarah K. Walker
Technical editors: Theresa Gaffey, Donna Druchunas, and Ellen Silva

Printed and bound in the United States of America

Produced by:
840 Books
840 Grand Avenue
Saint Paul, MN 55105

wearwithallbook.com

contents

introduction

You know the drill: you want to knit something new—something beautiful—so off you go in search of a pattern. From thousands of free patterns on the Internet to bookshelves loaded down with knitting inspiration—the sheer volume of material is overwhelming. Where do you start?

Our goal in creating *Wearwithall* is to give you the means (the wherewithal, if you will) to create a collection of knitwear with enough variety to make this book the one you come back to again and again. We offer designs that work, clothing that is both fashionable and timeless, projects that can be tailored to your family's lifestyle, and given confidently as gifts. If you're a beginning knitter, you'll find much to accomplish in this book. You'll follow clear, well-written patterns that give you great results. If you've been knitting longer than you care to admit, you'll be engaged by options to add more color, texture, and complexity to the patterns.

Theme and variations
The contents page of this book lists 13 patterns—from accessories to sweaters to blankets—and that's accurate. But dig a little deeper and you'll see that each pattern begets several more, simply by making small changes.

For instance, take a look at the mitten pattern. Gorgeous colorwork, right? But if stranded knitting overwhelms you, you can knit the version with a more manageable band of the colorwork at the cuff. Or consider the hat pattern: one stitch pattern produces both a man's and woman's version. A toddler sweater becomes a tunic, and a gorgeous stole shares its DNA with a classic rugby scarf. Best of all, you don't have to make these changes on your own. We walk you through each variation, both in these pages and at wearwithallbook.com.

A cooperative approach
How do five friends and colleagues come together to create a cohesive book? Forget the adage about too many cooks; we were convinced this was a collaboration that could work. We were inspired to create a truly useful book, and we knew that pooling our different talents could make that hope a reality. We engaged in months of critiquing designs, refining patterns, and choosing the right photos.

Selecting those photos was no easy matter, because we had so many great ones. When it came time to photograph our designs, only one name came to mind: Gale Zucker. Her clean, creative shots make the patterns pop, and her insight made our work better, every time. Her energy and wit made for a fun (and exhausting) photo shoot—we couldn't have asked for a better collaborator. Our designers, models, stylists, and test knitters were equally creative and enthusiastic, and our colleagues at The Yarnery in St. Paul, Minnesota (yarnery.com) were supportive and encouraging.

A cooperative approach may not seem to be the easiest or most efficient one, but it worked! And we think you'll like the result. Besides, we laughed. A lot.

Now it's your turn. Play with the designs you find here. Learn from the tips we've scattered throughout the book, and try the variations we've suggested in these pages and online. Speaking of online, remember to visit wearwithallbook.com, because we'll continue to play with these designs, too. When we think of a detail to add interest to the man's sweater, you'll be the first to know. When we come across a new yarn that's perfect for the cable cowl, we'll show you. And we hope you'll do the same: let us know what you come up with!

The five of us have enjoyed our collaboration every step of the way, but it's this next step—with you—that promises to be the most fun of all.

— Scott Rohr

socks

by Theresa Gaffey

Size

Adult small (medium, large)
Foot circumference around middle of foot: 8 (8 ½, 9 ¼)"
around. Length can be varied to fit individual foot.

Materials

Cascade 220 worsted-weight yarn from Cascade Yarns (220
yards per 100-gram skein): 2 skeins color A (Silver grey
#8401) and 1 skein each colors B (Charcoal grey #8400)
and C (Provence orange #2425)

1 set of double-pointed knitting needles size US 4 (3.5 mm)
(or one 40-inch circular knitting needles for magic loop
or two 20-inch circular knitting needles) or size needed to
obtain gauge
Blunt tapestry needle

Gauge

In stockinette st, 26 sts and 34 rows = 4"

Note: To keep the ribbing panels looking neat, gauge is
tighter than normal for worsted-weight yarn.

TO KNIT

With color B (charcoal grey), loosely cast on 52 (56, 60) sts
and separate them evenly onto 3 double-pointed knitting
needles. (If using circular needles, separate them onto two
circular needles or use magic loop.) Join into a circle, being
careful not to twist the first round. Place marker for beginning of round.
Work in k1, p1 rib for 6 rounds.

Begin side rib pattern

Next round: *K7 (7, 9) sts, (p1, k1) 6 times, p1, k6 (8, 8); rep
from * one more time.
Work 5 more rounds in pattern as established. Change to
color C (orange) and work 2 rounds in pattern. Change to
color A (silver grey) and work in pattern until piece
measures 7 ½ (8, 8 ½)" or desired length to heel.

Divide for heel

Distribute sts as follows: Knit the first 13 (13, 15) sts of next
round, slide the last 12 (14, 14) sts of previous round onto
the same needle. Redistribute the remaining 27 (29, 31) sts
onto 2 needles or a holder for the instep (top of foot).

Heel flap

Begin working back and forth.
Row 1 (WS): Slip first st knitwise, purl to end.

Row 2 (RS): *Slip 1 as if to purl, k1; repeat from * across to last 3 sts, slip 1, knit last 2 sts tog; 24 (26, 28) sts.
Row 3: Slip first st knitwise, purl to end.
Row 4: *Slip 1 as if to purl, k1; rep from * across.
Repeat rows 3 and 4 until heel flap measures 2 (2 ¼, 2 ½)", ending with a RS row.

Turn heel
Row 1 (WS): Slip 1, p12 (13, 14) sts, p2tog, p1, turn.
Row 2: Slip 1, k3, ssk, k1, turn.
Row 3: Slip 1, p4, p2tog, p1, turn.
Row 4: Slip 1, k5, ssk, k1, turn.
Row 5: Slip 1, p6, p2tog, p1, turn.

Continue in this manner, working one more st before the decrease on each row (which closes up the gap caused by the turn) until all sts are worked; 14 (14, 16) sts. End with a RS row.

Note: For the medium size, the last 2 rows end with p2tog or ssk. There is no final st after the decrease.

Gusset
With RS still facing, pick up and k12 (13, 14) sts along left edge of heel flap. Transfer instep sts (top of foot) from holder onto a needle and work pattern as established across top of foot, as follows: (p1, k1) 3 times, p1, k11 (13, 15), k2tog, (p1, k1) 3 times. With a third needle, pick up and k12 (13, 14) sts along other edge of heel flap and knit the first 7 (7, 8) sts of heel. Mark the middle of the heel as the beginning of round. You will have 19 (20, 22) sts on first needle, 26 (28, 30) sts on second needle, and 19 (20, 22) sts on third needle; 64 (68, 74) sts total.

Shape instep
Round 1: Work in pattern, continuing rib pattern on the instep stitches only. Work gussets and bottom of foot in stockinette st.

Round 2 (decrease round): Knit across first needle to last 2 sts, k2tog; work even in pattern across second needle; at beginning of third needle, ssk, knit to end of round.
Repeat these 2 rounds until you are back to 52 (56, 60) sts; 13 (14, 15) sts on first and third needles, 26 (28, 30) sts on second needle.

Foot
Work even as established until foot measures 8 (8 ½, 9)" or 2 (2, 2 ¼)" less than desired length, measured from back of heel. Break off color A.

Shape toe
Change to color B and stockinette st.
Round 1: Knit.
Round 2 (decrease round): Work to last 3 sts of first needle, k2tog, k1. On second needle, k1, ssk, knit to last 3 sts, k2tog, k1. On third needle, k1, ssk, knit to end of round.

Repeat these 2 rounds (decreasing every other round) until 20 sts remain. Then knit to end of first needle.

FINISHING
Break off yarn, leaving a 12" tail. Place sts of first and third needles onto one needle (10 sts on each of two needles). Graft toe with Kitchener stitch *(see appendix)*.

Weave in ends. Block.

These socks are quick and easy to knit with worsted-weight yarn. The side ribbing panels help them stretch and fit well, so your socks won't fall down while you're wearing them.

mittens

by Theresa Gaffey

Size

Adult small (medium, large, x-large)
Finished measurement around palm: 7 (7 ½, 8, 8 ½)"
These are snug-fitting mittens. Small will fit a woman's small hand; medium will fit a woman's medium hand, large will fit either a woman's large hand or a man's medium hand, x-large will fit most men's hands.

Materials

Alpaca Sport from Frog Tree Yarns (130 yards per 50-gram skein): 1 skein color A (Smoky purple #82) and 2 skeins each colors B (Deep teal #64) and C (Avocado green #46)
For grey mittens with patterned cuff: 2 skeins MC (Grey heather #009) and 1 skein CC (Smoky purple #82).
For purple mittens: 2 skeins MC (Smoky purple #82) and 1 skein CC (Brass #13)
For brown mittens: Felted Tweed from Rowan (191 yards per 50-gram skein): 2 skeins MC (Phantom brown #153) and 1 skein CC (Avocado green #161)

Double-pointed knitting needles size US 2 (3 mm) (or one 40-inch circular knitting needles for magic loop or two 20-inch circular knitting needles) or size needed to obtain gauge
Stitch markers
Stitch holder
Small tapestry needle

Gauge

In stockinette st and in color pattern or solid, 32 sts and 40 rows = 4"

Note: See page 12 for a photo of all variations.

TO KNIT

With color A (purple), cast on 56 (60, 64, 68) sts and separate evenly onto 3 double-pointed knitting needles. Join into circle, being careful not to twist the first round. Place marker for beginning of round.
Work in stockinette st (knit every round) for 6 rounds for rolled edge.
Change to color B (teal) and color C (green) and begin mitten chart.
Repeat chart until cuff measures 3" from last row of rolled edge or desired length to base of thumb gusset at wrist. End with a solid color round or some other reasonable place in the chart.

Begin thumb gusset

Note: Work thumb gusset chart (that is, 1 st color B, 1 st color C) over thumb sts, but continue main pattern as established for hand of mitten. Be aware that there will be an occasional solid color round in main pattern; work the solid color round across the thumb sts, too. Use backward loop style of M1 *(see appendix).*
Next round (row 1 of thumb gusset chart): K1 color B, place marker, M1 color C, place second marker, k1 color B, work remainder of round in mitten chart.

Note: Keep st before first marker and st after second marker in color B throughout.

Next 2 rounds: Work in color pattern as established.
Next round: K1 color B, slip marker, M1 color B, k1 color C, M1 color B, slip marker, k1 color B, work remainder of round in mitten chart.

Note: You are increasing **every third** round.

Continue to increase 1 st after first marker and 1 st before second marker, following the thumb gusset chart until there are 21 (23, 25, 25) sts between markers. Finish round.

Palm

Next round: K1, place thumb sts on holder, M1, knit remainder of round in mitten pattern.

Next round: K1, k2tog (at back of thumb), work in pattern; 56 (60, 64, 68) sts.

Continue in mitten pattern until palm measures 3 (3 ¼, 3 ½, 3 ¾)" above thumb or 1 ½ (1 ¾, 2, 2)" less than desired length.

Decrease for top

If you prefer to make decreasing easier, change to thumb gusset chart now.

Next round: *K1 color B, ssk with color C, knit in mitten chart over next 22 (24, 26, 28) sts, k2tog with color C, k1 with color B, place second marker; rep from * once more.

Note: Keep the first 2 and last 2 sts of each side of top in colors as established on this round (except for solid color rounds).

Next 2 rounds: Work even.

Next round: *K1 color B, ssk with color C, knit to last 3 sts before marker, k2tog with color C, k1 with color B; rep from * once more.

Work 2 rounds even.

Repeat these last 3 rounds 2 more times.

Change to thumb color pattern (1 st color B, 1 st color C) between decreases, and continue to decrease every other round 2 times as above, then decrease every round until 20 sts remain.

Break yarn, leaving a 10" tail of color B. Graft remaining sts together using Kitchener stitch *(see appendix)*.

Thumb

Place sts from holder onto 3 needles. Place marker for beginning of round, then pick up 1 st over the M1 st and

1 st on either side of it; 24 (26, 28, 28) sts. Continuing in thumb color pattern as established, work until thumb measures 1 ¾ (2, 2 ¼, 2 ½)" or ½" less than desired length.

Decrease for top
Note: Continue color pattern or change to color B.
For medium only: *K11, k2tog; rep from * once more;
24 (24, 28, 28) sts.
Round 1: *K2, k2tog; rep from * around; 18 (18, 21, 21) sts.
Round 2: Knit.
Round 3: *K1, k2tog; rep from * around; 12 (12, 14, 14) sts.
Round 4: *K2tog; rep from * around; 6 (6, 7, 7) sts.
Break yarn and draw tail through remaining sts to fasten off.

FINISHING
Weave in ends. Block.

VARIATIONS

For grey mittens with patterned cuff
Work rolled edge in purple. Then work mitten chart rows 1-20, then rows 1-9 again. Knit rest of mitten in grey. Shown in medium

For purple mittens
Work rolled edge in brass and rest of mitten with purple. Shown in small.

For brown mittens
Work 9 rounds of k2, p2 rib (4 rows green, 5 rows brown), then change to stockinette st and continue with brown for 5 rounds (½"). With green, work 10 rounds (about 1"). Work rest of mitten in brown. Shown in large.

legend
- ■ color B
- ▣ color C

mitten chart

thumb gusset chart
Continue to increase until there are 21 (23, 25) thumb stitches.

Note: Chart does not show solid colored rounds.

hats

by Martha Alvarado

Size
Woman's medium (man's medium)
Finished measurements: 21 ½" circumference for woman's slouchy hat; 19" for man's close-fitting hat

Materials
For woman's hat: Ultra Alpaca Light double-knitting weight yarn from Berroco (144 yards per 50-gram skein): 2 skeins (Turquoise mix #4294)

16-inch circular knitting needles size US 2 (3 mm) and size US 5 (3.75 mm) and double-pointed knitting needles size US 5 (3.75 mm)
Stitch markers

For man's hat: Ultra Alpaca worsted-weight yarn from Berroco (215 yards per 100-gram skein): 1 skein (Oregano green #6218)

16-inch circular knitting needles size US 4 (3.5 mm) and size US 7 (4.5 mm) and double-pointed knitting needles size US 7 (4.5 mm)
Stitch markers

Gauge
For woman's hat: In Eyelet Flemish Block stitch and Ultra Alpaca Light, using larger needles, 24 sts and 40 rows = 4"
For man's hat: In Flemish Block stitch and Ultra Alpaca worsted, using larger needles, 20 sts and 32 rows = 4"

PATTERN STITCHES
Note: Because of the nature of the decreases and increases in the Flemish Block and Eyelet Flemish Block patterns, there are 3 "selvedge" stitches at the back of hat where the pattern doesn't line up.

Eyelet Flemish Block pattern (woman's hat)
Round 1 (and all odd rounds): Knit.
Round 2: K2, *k2tog, yo, k1, yo, ssk, k3, k2tog, yo, k4; rep from * to last st, k1.
Round 4: K1, *k2tog, yo, k3, yo, ssk, k1, k2tog, yo, k4; rep from * to last 2 sts, k2.
Round 6: K2tog, yo, *k5, yo, sl1-k2tog-psso, yo, k4, k2tog, yo; rep from * to last st, k1.
Round 8: K2, *yo, ssk, k4, yo, ssk, k3, k2tog, yo, k1; rep from * to last st, k1.
Round 10: K3, *yo, ssk, k4, yo, ssk, k1, k2tog, yo, k3; rep from * to end.
Round 12: K4, *yo, ssk, k4, yo, k3tog, yo, k5; rep from * to end, end last repeat with k4.
Repeat rounds 1-12 for pattern.

Flemish Block pattern (man's hat)
Note: The man's version of the Flemish Block pattern uses M1 increases instead of yo eyelets.
Round 1 (and all odd rounds): Knit.
Round 2: K2, *k2tog, M1, k1, M1, ssk, k3, k2tog, M1, k4; rep from * to last st, k1.

Round 4: K1, *k2tog, M1, k3, M1, ssk, k1, k2tog, M1, k4; rep from * to last 2 sts, k2.
Round 6: K2tog, M1, *k5, M1, sl1-k2tog-psso, M1, k4, k2tog, M1; rep from * to last st, k1.
Round 8: K2, *M1, ssk, k4, M1, ssk, k3, k2tog, M1, k1; rep from * to last st, k1.
Round 10: K3, *M1, ssk, k4, M1, ssk, k1, k2tog, M1, k3; rep from * to end.
Round 12: K4, *M1, ssk, k4, M1, k3tog, M1, k5; rep from * to end, end last repeat with k4.
Repeat rounds 1-12 for pattern.

TO KNIT WOMAN'S HAT

With smaller needles, cast on 116 sts. Join into a circle, being careful not to twist the first round. Place marker for beginning of round.
Work k2, p2 rib for 1 ¼". Increase 13 sts in next round as follows: k8, M1, *k9, M1; rep from * to end; 129 sts. Change to larger needles and work rounds 1-12 of Eyelet Flemish Block pattern five times; hat measures approximately 8" from cast-on edge.

Shape top

Round 1 (and all odd rounds): Knit.
Round 2: K2, *k2tog, yo, k1, yo, ssk, k3, k2tog, k4; rep from * to last st, k1.
Note: There is no yo after the second k2tog in this and following rounds.
Round 4: K1, *k2tog, yo, k3, yo, ssk, k1, k2tog, k3; rep from * to last 2 sts, k2.
Round 6: K2tog, yo, *k5, yo, sl1-k2tog-psso, yo, k2, k2tog; rep from * to last st, k1; 102 sts.
Note: Discontinue pattern. Move beginning-of-round marker as follows: Slip marker off needle, knit first st, replace marker.
Round 8: K2tog, k8, k2tog, *k9, k2tog; rep from * to last 2 sts, k2tog.

Round 10: *K8, k2tog; rep from * to end, end last repeat with k3tog; 81 sts.
Round 12: *K7, k2tog; rep from * to end.
Round 14: *K6, k2tog; rep from * to end.
Continue to decrease every other round until 36 sts remain.
Begin to decrease every round until 9 sts remain. Break yarn and draw tail through remaining sts to fasten off.

TO KNIT MAN'S HAT

With smaller needles, cast on 96 sts. Join in the round, being careful not to twist. Place marker for beginning of round.
Work k2, p2 rib for 1". Increase 5 sts in next round as follows: *k19, M1; rep from * to last st, end k1; 101 sts. Change to larger needles and work rounds 1-12 of Flemish Block pattern three times; hat measures approximately 6" from cast-on edge.

Shape top

Round 1 (and all odd rounds): Knit.
Round 2: K2, *k2tog, M1, k1, M1, ssk, k3, k2tog, k4; rep from * to last st, k1.
Note: There is no M1 after the second k2tog in this and following rounds.
Round 4: K1, *k2tog, M1, k3, M1, ssk, k1, k2tog, k3; rep from * to last 2 sts, k2.
Round 6: K2tog, M1, *k5, M1, sl1-k2tog-psso, M1, k2, k2tog; rep from * to last st, k1; 80 sts.
Note: Discontinue pattern st. Move beginning-of-round marker as follows: slip marker off needle, knit first st, replace marker.
Round 8: K2tog, k8, k2tog, *k9, k2tog; rep from * to last 2 sts, k2tog.
Round 10: *K8, k2tog; rep from * to last 3 sts, k3tog; 63 sts.
Round 12: *K7, k2tog; rep from * to end.

Round 14: *K6, k2tog; rep from * to end.
Continue to decrease every other round until
28 sts remain.
Begin to decrease every round until 7 sts
remain. Break yarn and draw tail through
remaining sts to fasten off.

FINISHING
Weave in ends. Block.

This Flemish Block stitch pattern is fun, but challenging. You may want to use stitch markers to keep track of repeats; just note that you will need to move markers as the increases and decreases shift.

cable scarf and cowl

by Angela Paulson and Scott Rohr

Size

*Finished measurements: 6" wide by 75" long for scarf;
6" wide by 35" long for cowl*

Materials

*Scarf: Soufflé super chunky-weight yarn from Berroco
(54 yards per 50-gram skein): 4 balls (Cortina #9330)*

*Cowl: Chunky Alpaca chunky-weight yarn from Frog Tree
(109 yards per 100-gram skein): 2 skeins (Deep teal #64 or
Charcoal grey #0010)*

*Knitting needles size US 17 (12.75 mm) or size needed to
obtain gauge*
Row counter
Tapestry needle
2-inch button (cowl only)
Cable tool (a large double-pointed needle works well)

Gauge

*In k1, p1 rib (not stretched), 14 sts and 10 rows = 4" using 1
strand of Berroco Soufflé or 2 strands of Frog Tree Chunky
held double*

Ribbed cable pattern

Worked over 20 sts.

Rows 1-10: *K1, p1; rep from * to end. This establishes the
k1, p1 rib to be used throughout.

Row 11 (cable cross row): K1, p1, sl next 8 sts to cable tool,
hold in back. Work next 8 sts in k1, p1 rib. Work 8 sts from
cable tool in rib; end row with k1, p1.

Rows 12-28 (17 rows): Work in k1, p1 rib.

TO KNIT SCARF

With Soufflé, cast on 20 sts and work rows 1-28 of ribbed
cable pattern, then repeat rows 11-28 seven more times.
End scarf with rows 11-22 (9 cable crosses total).
Bind off all sts in pattern.

TO KNIT COWL

With Frog Tree Chunky held double, cast on 20 sts and
work rows 1-28 of ribbed cable pattern, then repeat rows
11-28 two more times, then work rows 11-22 (4 cable
crosses total).

Divide for split end

On next row, work in k1, p1 rib over first 10 sts; leaving
remaining sts on hold, turn work.
Working only these 10 sts, work 12 more rows in rib. Bind
off these sts in pattern. Break yarn.
Rejoin yarn at center where you left 10 unworked sts, and
work in rib for 9 rows.
Buttonhole row: Work first 6 sts in rib, bind off next st,
finish row in rib. On next row, M1 over bound-off st. Work
2 more rows. Bind off all sts in pattern on next row.

FINISHING

Weave in ends. For cowl, sew button to right side of split
end, opposite buttonhole.

To wear cowl: Drape cowl flat around neck with split end
over right shoulder. Insert button end through first (or
second) cable cross of left side, and secure.

stole

by Theresa Gaffey

Size
Finished measurements, after blocking: 29 ¼" wide by 80" long

Materials
Alpaca 2 fingering-weight yarn from Isager (275 yards per 50-gram skein): 1 skein each of 9 colors: color A (Old gold #3), B (Green grey #23), C (Marine blue-green #16), D (Orange #24), E (Dusty plum #52), F (Medium green #43), G (Medium natural brown #8s), H (Red #21), I (Chartreuse #40)

40-inch circular knitting needles size US 5 (3.75 mm) or size needed to obtain gauge
Tapestry needle

Gauge
In k8, p8 rib, 18 sts and 44 rows = 4", after blocking

K8, p8 rib pattern
Worked over a multiple of 16 sts plus 8.
Row 1: (K8, p8) to last 8 sts, k8.
Row 2: (P8, k8) to last 8 sts, p8.
Repeat rows 1-2 for rib pattern.

TO KNIT
With color A (gold), loosely cast on 360 sts.
Working in k8, p8 rib, work 36 rows (approximately 3 ¼" when stretched flat) of each color in following sequence: A, B, C, D, E, F, G, H, I (gold, green grey, blue-green, orange, plum, medium green, brown, red, chartreuse). After working all 9 colors, bind off loosely in pattern.

FINISHING
Weave in ends. Wash and dry flat to block (ribbing will relax). Edges will curl slightly.

rugby scarf
by Theresa Gaffey and Scott Rohr

Size
Finished measurements: 14" wide by 64" long

Materials
Eco Wool heavy worsted-weight yarn from Cascade Yarns (478 yards per 250-gram skein): 1 skein each of 4 colors: color A (Straw gold #4010), B (Gun metal grey #8020), C (Lichen green #9338), D (Night vision brown #8025)

Knitting needles size US 9 (5.5 mm) or size needed to obtain gauge
Tapestry needle

Gauge
In k6, p6 rib, 16 sts and 20 rows = 4"

K6, p6 rib pattern
Worked over a multiple of 12 sts plus 6.
Row 1: (K6, p6) to last 6 sts, k6.
Row 2: (P6, k6) to last 6 sts, p6.
Repeat rows 1-2 for rib pattern.

TO KNIT
With color A (gold), cast on 54 stitches. Working in k6, p6 rib, work 22 rows of each color in the following sequence: A, B, C, A, D, C (gold, grey, green, gold, brown, green). Repeat color sequence one more time, then end scarf with colors A, B, C, A (gold, grey, green, gold) in that order. Bind off in rib pattern.

FINISHING
Weave in ends. Wash and dry flat to block (ribbing will relax). Edges will curl slightly.

blanket

by Theresa Gaffey

Size

Finished measurements: Baby blanket measures 30" square; afghan measures 60" square

Materials

For baby blanket: Handknit Cotton worsted-weight yarn from Rowan (93 yards per 50-gram skein): 2 skeins each of 5 colors: color A (Ice water blue #239), B (Gooseberry lime #219), C (Ochre yellow #349), D (Sea foam green #352), E (Delphinium purple #334)

For afghan: Ultra Alpaca worsted-weight yarn from Berroco (215 yards per 100-gram skein): 4 skeins each of 4 main colors: color A (Couscous cream #6208), B (Buckwheat brown #6204), C (Dark chocolate brown #6205), D (Duncan brown #6211), and 2 skeins of border color E (Turquoise mix #6294)

32-inch circular knitting needles size US 8 (5 mm) for triangles, or size needed to obtain gauge

For baby blanket border: 40-inch or 60-inch circular knitting needles size US 8 (5 mm)

For afghan border: Two 40-inch or 60-inch circular knitting needles size US 8 (5 mm); the longer the better

Tapestry needle

Waste yarn to hold stitches

Gauge

In garter st, 18 sts and 34 rows (17 ridges) = 4"

TO KNIT

Note: For the baby blanket, knit 4 triangles, then sew them into a square and add the border. For the afghan, knit 16 triangles (4 of each color), then sew 1 triangle of each color into a square, then sew the 4 squares together and knit the border.

With color A (blue for baby blanket, cream for afghan), cast on 2 sts.

Row 1 (RS): Knit in front and back of first st (increasing one st), M1, knit last st; 4 sts.

Row 2: P1, knit to last st, p1.

Row 3: K1, M1, knit to last st, M1, k1.

Row 4: P1, knit to last st, p1.

Repeat rows 3 and 4 until there are 122 sts. The height of triangle is approximately 14".

For baby blanket: Place all sts on a holder. Work 3 more triangles, one of each main color.

For afghan: Bind off all sts. Leave a 36" tail for sewing together. Work 4 triangles in each of the 4 main colors.

FINISHING

For baby blanket

Using mattress stitch, sew the 4 triangles together.

To knit border: Move stitches from holders onto longer circular needle, placing a marker at each corner.

Next round: *K1, M1, knit to 1 st before next corner

marker, M1, k1; rep from * to beginning of round. You are increasing 2 sts at each corner; 8 sts total. Purl 1 round. Continue working in garter st (knit 1 round, purl 1 round), increasing on every knit round until border measures 1 ¼" (6 ridges). Bind off on next RS round.

Weave in ends.

For afghan
Using mattress stitch, sew 4 triangles (1 of each color) together into a square. Repeat for other triangles, keeping colors in same sequence. You will have 4 squares.
Sew squares together, rotating the squares to form a pinwheel when all squares are sewn together.

To knit border: Using 2 long circular needles, pick up and k240 sts along each side, placing a marker at each corner. Next round: *K1, M1, knit to 1 st before next corner marker, M1, k1; rep from * to beginning of round. You are increasing 2 sts at each corner; 8 sts total. Purl 1 round. Continue working in garter st (knit 1 round, purl 1 round), increasing on every knit round until there are 10 ridges. Bind off on next RS round.

Weave in ends.

This blanket is a surprisingly portable project. Each triangle is knit separately and joined to make a square. To make the blanket or afghan larger or smaller, simply add or subtract rows.

Take some time to play with the squares in the afghan. Turn them until you like the pattern you've made. See some possible configurations below.

afghan layout variations

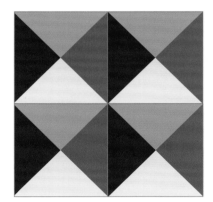

baby sweater and tunic

by Mary Lou Egan

Size

Baby sizes 3-6 months (6-12 months, 12-24 months)
Finished chest circumference: 18 (20 ½, 24)"
Length: 11 (12 ½, 14 ½)" for sweater; 14 (15 ½, 17 ½)" for tunic

Materials

Cascade 220 Superwash Sport from Cascade Yarns (136 yards per 50-gram skein)
For sweater: 2 (3, 4) skeins of MC (Denim blue #845) and 1 skein of CC (Green apple #802)
For tunic: 3 (4, 5) skeins of MC (Green apple #802) and 1 skein of CC (Coral #827)

Knitting needles size US 2 (2.75 mm) and size US 4 (3.5mm) or size needed to obtain gauge
Split ring or safety pin style markers
Blunt tapestry needle

Gauge

In stockinette st with larger needles, 24 sts and 36 rows = 4"

Note: Instructions for tunic are at end of the pattern.

TO KNIT
SWEATER BACK

With smaller needles and CC (green), cast on 54 (62, 72) sts. Knit 6 rows. Change to larger needles and MC (blue). Beginning with a knit row, work in stockinette st (knit 1 row, purl 1 row) until piece measures 7 (8, 9)" from cast-on edge.

Shape armholes

Bind off 4 (4, 6) sts at beginning of next 2 rows; 46 (54, 60) sts. Continue in stockinette st until back measures 9 (10 ½, 12)" from cast-on edge, ending with a WS row.
Next row (RS): K19 (22, 24) sts (place these sts on holder), bind off center 8 (10, 12) sts, k19 (22, 24) sts.

Shape left back shoulder (as worn) and neck

Row 1 (WS): Purl to last 2 sts, p2tog.
Row 2: Bind off 1 st, knit to end of row.
Repeat these 2 rows 3 more times, then rep row 1 once more; 10 (13, 15) sts remain. Work 8 (10, 14) rows even. Place split ring marker at outer edge of last row to mark top of shoulder.

Shape shoulder overlap

Bind off 1 st at neck edge on next 2 RS rows, then bind off 2 sts at the neck edge on the next 2 RS rows, then bind off 3 sts at neck edge on the next RS row. Bind off remaining 1 (4, 6) sts.

Shape right back shoulder (as worn) and neck

With WS facing, place sts from holder onto needle and join MC at neck edge.

Row 1 (WS): Bind off 1 st, purl to end of row.

Row 2: Knit to last 2 sts, k2tog.

Repeat these 2 rows 3 more times, then rep row 1 once more; 10 (13, 15) sts remain. Work 8 (10, 14) rows even. Place split ring marker at outer edge of last row to mark top of shoulder.

Shape shoulder overlap

Bind off 1 st at neck edge on next 2 WS rows, then bind off 2 sts at neck edge on next 2 WS rows, then bind off 3 sts at neck edge on next WS row. Bind off remaining 1 (4, 6) sts.

Neck edging

With smaller needles and CC, pick up and k59 (65, 72) sts along top edge of back, knit 3 rows, bind off. *Note:* Do not wait until sweater is seamed to knit neck edging.

SWEATER FRONT

Work as for back until armhole shaping is finished. Continue to work in stockinette st until piece measures 8 ½ (10, 11 ½)" from cast-on edge, ending with a WS row. K19 (22, 24) sts (place these sts on holder), bind off center 8 (10, 12) sts, k19 (22, 24) sts.

Shape right front shoulder (as worn) and neck

Row 1 (WS): Purl to last 2 sts, p2tog.

Row 2: Bind off 1 st, knit to end of row.

Repeat these 2 rows 3 more times, then repeat row 1 once more; 10 (13, 15) sts remain. Work 12 (14, 16) rows even. Place split ring markers at outer edge of last row to mark top of shoulder.

Shape shoulder overlap

Bind off 1 st at neck edge on next 2 RS rows, then bind off 2 sts at neck edge on next 2 RS rows, then bind off 3 sts at neck edge on next WS row. Bind off remaining 1 (4, 6) sts.

Shape left front shoulder (as worn) and neck

With WS facing, place sts from holder onto needle and join MC at neck edge.

Row 1: (WS) Bind off 1 st, purl to end of row.

Row 2: Knit to last 2 sts, k2tog.

Repeat these 2 rows 3 more times, then repeat row 1 once more; 10 (13, 15) sts remain. Work 12 (14, 16) rows even. Place split ring marker at outer edge of last row to mark top of shoulder.

Shape shoulder overlap

Bind off 1 st at neck edge on next 2 WS rows, then bind off 2 sts at neck edge on next 2 WS rows, then bind off 3 sts at neck edge on next WS row. Bind off remaining 1 (4, 6) sts.

Neck edging

With smaller needles and CC, pick up and k62 (68, 76) sts along top edge of front, knit 3 rows, bind off.

SLEEVES

Note: Sleeves are worked from the top down before sewing side seams.

Overlap back shoulders over front shoulders, matching markers. Overlap should extend equally down front and back. Armhole should measure 8 (9, 11)" between the bound-off armhole shaping sections on the front and the back; adjust overlap as needed.

With larger needles, MC and RS facing, pick up and k48 (54, 66) sts along armhole, going through both thicknesses at shoulders. Do not pick up along bound-off edge of underarm. Beginning with a purl row, work 9 (7, 7) rows in stockinette st.

Shape sleeve

Next row (RS): K2, k2tog, knit to last 4 sts, ssk, k2;

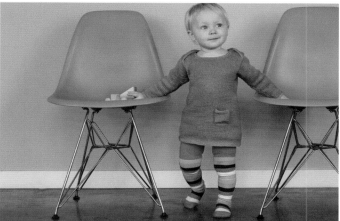

continue to decrease every 8 (8, 10) rows 5 (6, 6) more times; 36 (40, 52) sts remain. Work even, if needed, until sleeve measures 6 ½ (7 ½, 8 ½)" from pick-up, ending with a WS row.

Cuff
Change to smaller needles and CC, knit 3 rows. Bind off. Repeat for other sleeve.

FINISHING
Sew armhole bind-off to edge of sleeve. Sew underarm and side seams. Weave in ends. Block garment.

TUNIC BACK
With smaller needles and CC (coral), cast on 70 (80, 92) sts. Knit 6 rows. Change to larger needles and MC (green). Beginning with a knit row, work in stockinette st for 4 rows. Next row (RS): k2, k2tog, knit to last 4 sts, ssk, k2; continue to decrease every 8 (8, 10) rows 7 (8, 9) more times; 54 (62, 72) sts. Work even until piece measures 10 (11, 12)" from cast-on edge or desired length to underarm.

Shape armholes
Bind off 4 (4, 6) sts at beginning of next 2 rows; 46 (54, 60) sts.

Continue in stockinette st until back measures 12 (13 ½, 15)" from cast-on edge, ending with a WS row.
Next row (RS): K19 (22, 24) sts (place these sts on holder), bind off center 8 (10, 12) sts, k19 (22, 24) sts.

Shape left back shoulder (as worn) and neck
Row 1 (WS): Purl to last 2 sts, p2tog.
Row 2: Bind off 1 st, knit to end of row.
Repeat these 2 rows 3 more times, then rep row 1 once more; 10 (13, 15) sts remain. Work 8 (10, 14) rows even. Place split ring marker at outer edge of last row to mark top of shoulder.

Shape shoulder overlap
Bind off 1 st at neck edge on next 2 RS rows, then bind off 2 sts at neck edge on next 2 RS rows, then bind off 3 sts at neck edge on next WS row. Bind off remaining 1 (4, 6) sts.

Shape right back shoulder (as worn) and neck
With WS facing, place sts from holder onto needle and join MC at neck edge.
Row 1 (WS): Bind off 1 st, purl to end of row.
Row 2: Knit to last 2 sts, k2tog.
Repeat these 2 rows 3 more times, then rep row 1 once more;

10 (13, 15) sts remain. Work 8 (10, 14) rows even. Place split ring marker at outer edge of last row to mark top of shoulder.

Shape shoulder overlap
Bind off 1 st at neck edge on next 2 WS rows, then bind off 2 sts at neck edge on next 2 WS rows, then bind off 3 sts at neck edge on next WS row. Bind off remaining 1 (4, 6) sts.

Neck edging
With smaller needles and CC, pick up and k59 (65, 72) sts along top edge of back, knit 3 rows, bind off. *Note:* Do not wait until sweater is seamed to knit neck edging.

TUNIC FRONT
Work as for tunic back until armhole shaping is finished. Continue in stockinette st until piece measures 11 ½ (13, 14 ½)" from cast-on edge, ending with a WS row. K19 (22, 24) sts (place these sts on holder), bind off center 8 (10, 12) sts, k19 (22, 24) sts.

Shape left back shoulder (as worn) and neck
Row 1 (WS): Purl to last 2 sts, p2tog.
Row 2: Bind off 1 st, knit to end of row.
Repeat these 2 rows 3 more times, then rep row 1 once more; 10 (13, 15) sts remain. Work 8 (10, 14) rows even. Place split ring marker at outer edge of last row to mark top of shoulder.

Shape shoulder overlap
Bind off 1 st at neck edge on next 2 RS rows, then bind off 2 sts at the neck edge on the next 2 RS rows, then bind off 3 sts at neck edge on the next RS row. Bind off remaining 1 (4, 6) sts.

Shape right back shoulder (as worn) and neck
With WS facing, place sts from holder onto needle and join MC at neck edge.
Row 1 (WS): Bind off 1 st, purl to end of row.
Row 2: Knit to last 2 sts, k2tog.
Repeat these 2 rows 3 more times, then rep row 1 once more; 10 (13, 15) sts remain. Work 8 (10, 14) rows even. Place split ring marker at outer edge of last row to mark top of shoulder.

Shape shoulder overlap
Bind off 1 st at neck edge on next 2 WS rows, then bind off 2 sts at neck edge on next 2 WS rows, then bind off 3 sts at neck edge on next WS row. Bind off remaining 1 (4, 6) sts.

Neck edging
With smaller needles and CC, pick up and k59 (65, 72) sts along top edge of back, knit 3 rows, bind off.

TUNIC SLEEVES
Work sleeves as for sweater.

FINISHING
Sew armhole bind-off to edge of sleeve. Sew underarm and side seams. Weave in ends. Block garment.

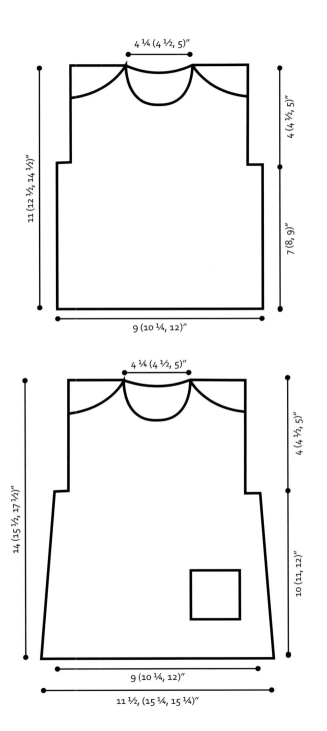

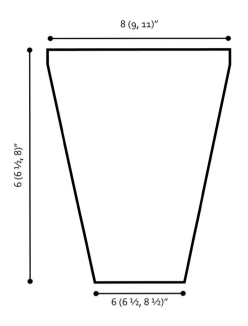

4 ¼ (4 ½, 5)"

4 (4 ½, 5)"

11 (12 ½, 14 ½)"

7 (8, 9)"

9 (10 ¼, 12)"

8 (9, 11)"

6 (6 ½, 8)"

6 (6 ½, 8 ½)"

4 ¼ (4 ½, 5)"

4 (4 ½, 5)"

14 (15 ½, 17 ½)"

10 (11, 12)"

9 (10 ¼, 12)"

11 ½, (15 ¼, 15 ¼)"

POCKET
A pocket can be made and placed on the front of either the tunic or the sweater for a cute addition.

With larger needles and MC, cast on 15 sts, work in stockinette st for 20 rows. Change to smaller needles and CC and knit 4 rows; bind off. Sew in place.

For another detail, please visit wearwithallbook.com.

toddler's cardigan

by Gretchen Funk

Size

Child's size 2 (4, 6) to fit chest measurement 21 (23, 25)"
Finished chest circumference: 24 ¼ (26 ¼, 28 ¼)", buttoned
Length: 13 ½ (15, 17)"

Materials

Meriboo MW worsted-weight yarn from Frog Tree (105 yards per 50-gram skein): 3 (3, 4) skeins color A and 2 (3, 3) skeins each of colors B and C
For green version: Color A (Forest #7045), color B (Pistachio #7046), color C (Sage #7405)
For purple version: Color A (Purple #7501), color B (Smoky lavender #7082), color C (Pistachio green #7046)

Straight or 24-inch circular knitting needles size US 5 (3.75 mm) or size needed to obtain gauge
Double-pointed knitting needles size US 5 (3.75 mm) (or 40-inch circular knitting needles for magic loop)
8 stitch markers
2 stitch holders
Split ring or coiless safety pin style markers
5 buttons
Sewing needle and matching thread

Gauge

In garter st, 20 sts and 42 rows (21 ridges) = 4 "

TO KNIT

Beginning at neck with color A (forest or purple), cast on 44 (48, 51) sts.
Set-up row (WS): Sl first st purlwise wyif, k5 (6, 7) for right front, pm, p2, pm, k6 (7, 7) for right sleeve, pm, p2, pm, k12 (12, 13) for back, pm, p2, pm, k6 (7, 7) for left sleeve, pm, p2, pm, k6 (7, 8) for left front.
Follow chart for stripe pattern, starting with row 1.
Change colors on RS rows and *at the same time*, begin shaping as follows:

Raglan increase rows

Row 1 (RS): Slip first st purlwise wyif, *knit to 1 st before m, kfb, sl m, k2, sl m, kfb, rep from * a total of 4 times, knit to end.
Note: You are increasing before and after each marker, 8 sts added every increase row.
Row 2 (WS): Slip first st purlwise wyif, *knit to m, sl m, p2, sl m, rep from * a total of 4 times, knit to end.
Note: Knit all sts except the 2 raglan "seam" sts in between the markers.
Repeat these 2 rows 21 (22, 24) more times. End with a WS row.
Next row (sizes 4 and 6 only): Omit the increases on the sleeves: Slip first st purlwise wyif, knit to 1 st before m, kfb, sl m, k2, sl m, knit to next m, sl m, k2, sl m, kfb, knit to 1 st before next m, kfb, sl m, k2, sl m, knit to m, sl m, k2, sl m, kfb, knit to end; 4 sts increased. Work row 2 one more time to be on the RS of work.
For all sizes: 220 (236, 255) sts.

Separate sleeves and body

Remove markers as you come to them. Slip first st purlwise wyif, k28 (31, 34) front sts, put the next 52 (55, 59) sleeve sts without working them onto waste yarn or a holder, k58 (62, 67) back sts, put the next 52 (55, 59) sleeve sts without working them onto waste yarn or a holder, k29 (32, 35) front sts.

Work 116 (126, 137) sts of body in garter st, slipping the first stitch as established, for 9 (10, 11 ½)". Bind off loosely.

SLEEVES

Note: Please read through all sleeve instructions before beginning. Work in stripe pattern as for body.

Place the 52 (55, 59) sts of first sleeve onto double-pointed needles, pm, and join. Starting with a knit round, begin working garter st in the round (k1 round, p1 round). Work 4 rounds, then decrease on next round as follows (this is a RS round): K1, k2tog, knit to last 3 sts, ssk, k1.

Continue working garter st in the round and at same time, decrease 2 sts as established every 12 (16, 16) rounds, until 38 (39, 41) sts remain.

If needed, continue working without decreasing until sleeve measures 8 ½ (10 ½, 11 ½)" from underarm, or as long as desired. Bind off loosely.

Repeat for second sleeve.

FINISHING

Buttonband: Beginning at bottom edge with RS facing and with color A (forest or purple), pick up and k1 st for every ridge on right-front edge (as worn). Work in garter st for 8 rows (4 ridges). Bind off in knit on WS.

Buttonhole band: Along left-front edge, place a pin ½" from the top and another ½" from the bottom, then place 3 more pins evenly spaced between these. Beginning at top edge with right-side facing and with color A, pick up and work as for left-front edge for 3 rows (2 ridges). On next row (RS), work 5 buttonholes along edge as follows: knit first 4 sts, bind off next 2 sts, *knit to next pin, bind off 2 sts; rep from * 3 more times. Knit remaining sts. On next row, cast on 2 sts over bound-off sts. Knit 3 more rows. Bind off on next WS row.

Collar (optional)

With WS facing (so that pick-up ridge will be covered up by collar when it folds over) and color A, pick up and k53 (55, 60) sts along neck edge. Work in garter st for 16 rows (8 ridges). Bind off on next WS row.

Weave in ends. Block garment. Sew on buttons.

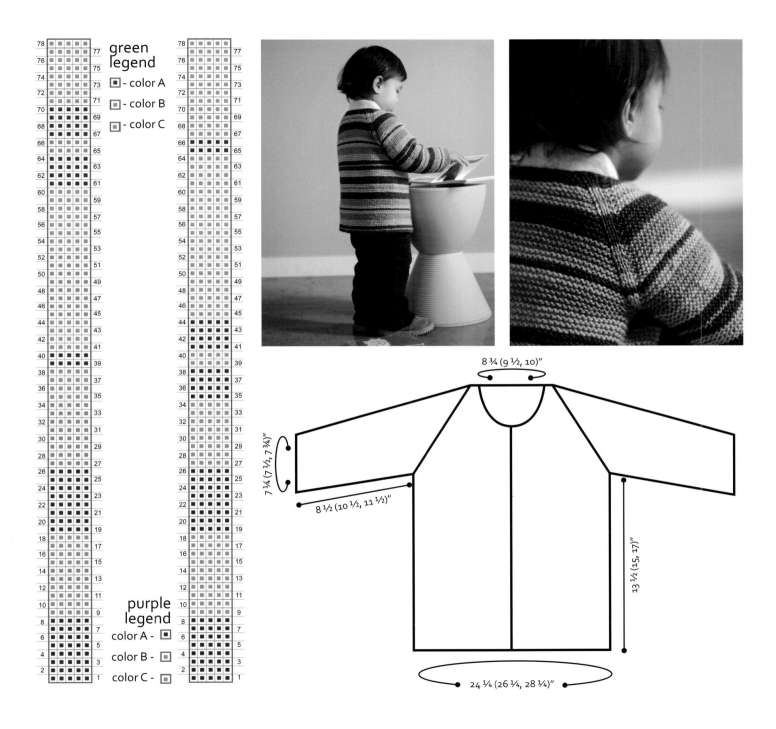

green
legend

■ - color A
□ - color B
□ - color C

purple
legend

color A - ■
color B - □
color C - □

8 ¾ (9 ½, 10)"

7 ¼ (7 ½, 7 ¾)"

8 ½ (10 ½, 11 ½)"

13 ½ (15, 17)"

24 ¼ (26 ¼, 28 ¼)"

child's vest

by Sarah K. Walker

Sizes

Child's size 4 (6, 8, 10) years
Finished chest circumference: 25 (27, 29, 31)"
Length: 14 ¼ (16 ¼, 18 ¼, 20 ¼)"

Materials

Cascade 220 Sport from Cascade Yarns (164 yards per 50-gram skein)
For grey version: 3 (4, 4, 5) skeins color A (Silver grey #8401) and 1 skein each colors B (Straw gold #4010) and C (Colonial blue heather #9326)
For aqua version: 3 (4, 4, 5) skeins color A (Lake Chelan heather aqua #9451) and 1 skein each colors B (Turtle green #2452) and C (Rainer heather purple #9454)
For plain blue version with contrast trim: 3 (4, 4, 5) skeins of color A (Colonial blue heather #9326) and 1 skein color B (Straw gold #4010)

Straight knitting needles size US 4 (3.5 mm) and size US 6 (4 mm) or size needed to obtain gauge
16-inch circular knitting needles size US 4 (3.5 mm) for neck and armholes
6 stitch holders
Bobbins
Tapestry needle

Gauge

In stockinette st with larger needles, 24 sts and 32 rows = 4"

TO KNIT

Note: See variation for plain vest at end of pattern.

BACK

With color A (grey or aqua) and smaller needles, cast on 75 (81, 87, 93) sts. Begin rib as follows:
Row 1: K2, *P1, K1, repeat from * to end.
Row 2: P2, *K1, P1, repeat from * to end.
Repeat these 2 rows 5 more times (12 rows total).
Change to larger needles and work in stockinette st for 4 rows.

Begin chart

Note: If you prefer, you can duplicate st the diagonal lines on chart using color C (blue or purple).

Work all rows of chart and then continue with color A until piece measures 9 (10, 11, 12)" from cast-on edge.

Shape armholes

At the beginning of next 2 rows, bind off 5 sts. Then at the beginning of the following 2 rows, bind off 3 sts; 59 (65, 71, 77) sts.
Next RS row: K1, ssk, knit to last 3 sts, k2tog, k1. Continue to decrease every other row 3 more times; 51 (57, 63, 69) sts remain.
Work even until piece measures 14 (16, 18, 20)" from cast-on edge, ending with a WS row.

Shape back neck and shoulders

Note: Work each side separately.

On next RS row, k14 (16, 18, 20) sts, k2tog, k1, and put these 16 (18, 20, 22) sts on a holder. Knit across center 17 (19, 21, 23) sts and place sts on a separate holder for neck.

Shape left back neck edge

Work on remaining 17 (19, 21, 23) sts as follows: K1, ssk, knit to end. Purl 1 row. Continue to decrease every other row at neck edge 4 more times; 12 (14, 16, 18) sts remain. Purl 1 row. Place these sts on holder for shoulder; break yarn.

Note: These sts will be joined to front shoulder sts with three-needle bind-off.

Shape right back neck edge

With WS facing, join yarn to the other shoulder; 16 (18, 20, 22) sts. Purl 1 row. On next RS row, knit to last 3 sts, k2tog, k1. Purl 1 row. Continue to decrease every other row at neck edge 3 more times; 12 (14, 16, 18) sts remain. Place sts on a holder for shoulder; break yarn.

FRONT

Work as for back until piece measures 12 (14, 16, 18)" from cast-on edge.

Shape front neck and shoulders

Note: Work each side separately.

On the next RS row, work first 19 (21, 23, 25) sts and place them on a holder. Work across center 13 (15, 17, 19) sts and place on a separate holder for neck.

Shape right front (as worn) neck edge

On remaining 19 (21, 23, 25) sts, work as follows: bind off 3 sts, knit to end. Purl 1 row. On next row, bind off 2 sts, knit to end. Purl 1 row. On next 2 RS rows: k1, ssk, knit to end; 12 (14, 16, 18) sts remain.

Work even until piece measures same as back to shoulder. Place remaining sts on holder.

Shape left front (as worn) neck edge

Place first 19 (21, 23, 25) sts back on needle and with WS facing, join yarn at neck edge and shape neck as follows: Bind off 3 sts, purl to end. Knit 1 row. Bind off 2 sts on next row, purl to end. On next 2 RS rows, knit to last 3 sts, k2tog, k1; 12 (14, 16, 18) sts remain.

Work even until piece measures same as back. Place sts on holder for shoulder.

FINISHING

Using the three-needle bind-off, join shoulders together. Seam sides of vest.

child's vest color chart

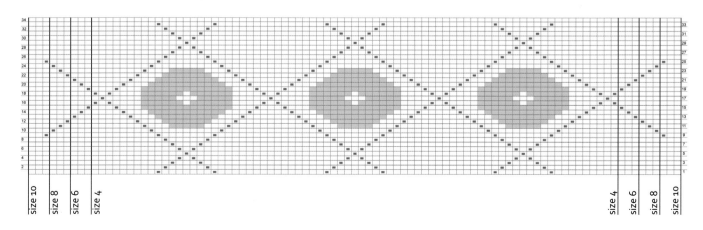

Neckband

With smaller circular needles, beginning at back of neck and with RS facing, knit across 17 (19, 21, 23) sts from back neck holder. Pick up and k24 (26, 28, 30) sts along left side of neck, knit across 13 (15, 17, 19) sts from front neck holder. Pick up and k24 (26, 28, 30) sts along the right side of neck; 78 (86, 94, 102) total sts. Place marker for beginning of round.

Work 6 rounds in k1, p1 ribbing. Bind off loosely.

Armhole bands

With smaller circular needles and beginning at underarm, pick up and k74 (80, 86, 92) sts around armhole edge. Place marker for beginning of round. Work 4 rounds in k1, p1 ribbing. Bind off loosely. Repeat for second armhole.

Weave in ends. Block garment.

FOR PLAIN VEST

For front and back, cast on with color B (gold) and work 1 row in k1, p1 rib. Change to color A (blue) and finish piece. For neckband, pick up with color A and work last row in color B (gold) and bind off.

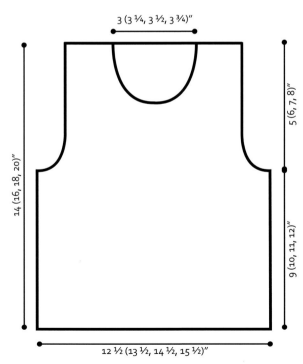

3 (3 ¼, 3 ½, 3 ¾)"

5 (6, 7, 8)"

14 (16, 18, 20)"

9 (10, 11, 12)"

12 ½ (13 ½, 14 ½, 15 ½)"

woman's cardigan

by Mary Lou Egan

Sizes

Woman's x-small (small, medium, large, x-large)
Finished bust circumference: 34 (36, 39, 42, 46)", buttoned

Materials

Kidsilk Haze version: Kidsilk Haze from Rowan (229 yards
per 25-gram skein): 6 (7, 8) skeins Majestic #589
Pediboo version: Pediboo from Frog Tree (255 yards per 100-
gram skein): 6 (7, 8) skeins MC (Smoky lilac #1182) and 1
skein CC (Charcoal #1110) (for contrast trim only)
Euroflax version: Euroflax from Louet (270 yards per 100-
gram skein): 6 (7, 8) skeins Steel grey #68

Knitting needles size US 2 (2.75 mm) and size US 4 (3.5 mm)
or size needed to obtain gauge
Blunt tapestry needle
Split ring markers
8 buttons
Sewing needle and matching thread

Gauge

In stockinette st with larger needles, 24 sts and 36 rows = 4"

Note: See variation for mitered band version at end of pattern.

TO KNIT
BACK

With smaller needles, cast on 104 (118, 126, 134, 146) sts.
Work in k1, p1 rib for 12 rows.
Change to larger needles and beginning with a knit row,
work in stockinette st (k 1 row, p 1 row) for 6 rows.

Shape waist

Decrease row: K2, k2 tog, knit to last 4 sts, ssk, k2; repeat
every 6 rows 7 more times; 88 (102, 110, 118, 130) sts. Purl
1 row. Work 20 rows even for waist, ending with a WS row.
Increase row: k2, LLI, knit to last 3 sts, RLI, k2; repeat
every 16 rows 3 more times; 96 (110, 118, 126, 138) sts.
Work even until piece measures 14 ¼ (14 ½, 15, 15 ½,
15 ½)" from cast-on edge or desired length to underarm.

Shape armholes

Bind off 4 (4, 6, 7, 8) sts at beginning of next 2 rows.
Bind off 1 st at beginning of next 4 rows; 84 (98, 102, 108,
118) sts.
Decrease 1 st at each end of needle on the next RS row,
then every 4 rows 4 (4, 4, 5, 7) more times; 74 (88, 92, 96,
102) sts.
Work even until armhole measures 7 ½ (8 ¼, 8 ½, 9, 9 ¼)"
from first bind-off row, ending with a WS row.

Shape left back neck (as worn) and shoulders

At beginning of next row, k29 (36, 37, 39, 41), bind off 16 (16, 18, 18, 20) sts for back neck, knit remaining 29 (36, 37, 39, 41) sts. Purl 1 row.
Note: Work each side of neck separately.

Bind off 5 sts at neck edge; 24 (31, 32, 34, 36) sts.
On next row, bind off 5 sts for shoulder; 19 (26, 27, 29, 31) sts.
Bind off 5 sts at neck edge; 14 (21, 22, 24, 26) sts.
Bind off 5 sts at shoulder; 9 (16, 17, 19, 21) sts.
Bind off 1 st at neck edge; 8 (15, 16, 18, 20) sts.
Bind off 5 sts at shoulder; 3 (10, 11, 13, 15) sts
For x-small only: Bind off remaining 3 sts.
Note: There is no more shaping for x-small size.

For larger sizes only:
Bind off 1 st at neck edge; – (9, 10, 12, 14) sts.
Bind off 5 sts at shoulder; – (4, 5, 7, 9) sts.
Bind off remaining sts.

Shape right back neck (as worn) and shoulders

Attach yarn at shoulder edge and knit across. Continuing in stockinette st, shape as for left neck and shoulder.

RIGHT FRONT (as worn)

With smaller needles, cast on 50 (57, 61, 65, 71) sts. Work in k1, p1 rib for 12 rows.
Change to larger needles and work 6 rows in stockinette st.

Shape waist

Decrease row: Knit to last 4 sts, ssk, k2; rep every 6 rows 7 more times; 42 (49, 53, 57, 63) sts. Purl 1 row.
Work 20 rows even for waist, ending with a WS row.
Increase row: Knit to last 3 sts, RLI; rep every 16 rows 3 more times; 46 (53, 57, 61, 67) sts.
Work even until piece measures 14 ¼ (14 ½, 15, 15 ½, 15 ½)" from cast-on edge or desired length to underarm.

Shape armhole

Bind off 4 (4, 6, 7, 8) sts at beginning of next WS row. Then bind off 1 st at beginning of following 2 WS rows; 40 (47, 49, 52, 57) sts.

Decrease row: Knit to last 4 sts, ssk, k2; rep every 4 rows 5 (5, 5, 6, 8) more times; 35 (42, 44, 46, 49) sts.
Work even until armhole measures 3 ½ (4 ¼, 4 ½, 5, 5 ¼)" or 4" less than back to shoulder shaping from cast-on edge.

Shape neck

Next RS row: Bind off 5 (5, 6, 6, 7) sts at neck edge; 30 (37, 38, 40, 42) sts. Purl 1 row.
Next row: Bind off 4 sts at neck edge. Purl 1 row.
Bind off 3 sts at neck edge at beginning of next RS row; 23 (30, 31, 33, 35) sts. Purl 1 row.
Bind off 1 st at neck edge every other row on RS 5 (6, 6, 6, 6) times; 18 (24, 25, 27, 29) sts.
Work even until front measures same as back to shoulder shaping.

Shape shoulder

At beginning of next 3 (4, 4, 4, 4) WS rows, bind off 5 sts.
Next WS row: Bind off remaining 3 (4, 5, 7, 9) sts.

LEFT FRONT (as worn)

Work as for right front, shaping waist as follows:
Work waist decreases: k2, k2tog, work to end of row.
Work waist increases: k2, LLI, work to end of row. Work until piece measures same as right front to underarm.

Shape armhole

Bind off 4 (4, 6, 7, 8) sts at beginning of next RS row.
Bind off 1 st at beginning of following 2 RS rows; 40 (47, 49, 52, 57) sts.
Decrease row: K2, k2tog, knit across; rep every 4 rows at armhole edge 5 (5, 5, 6, 8) more times.
Work even until piece measures 4" less than back from cast-on edge.

Shape neck

Next WS row: Bind off 5 (5, 6, 6, 7) sts at neck edge; 30 (37, 38, 40, 42) sts. Knit 1 row.
Next row: Bind off 4 sts at neck edge. Knit 1 row.
Bind off 3 sts at neck edge; 23 (30, 31, 33, 35) sts. Knit 1 row.

Bind off 1 st at neck edge every other row on WS 5 (6, 6, 6, 6) times; 18 (24, 25, 27, 29) sts.
Work even until front measures same as back to shoulder shaping.

Shape shoulder
At beginning of next 3 (4, 4, 4, 4) RS rows, bind off 5 sts.
Next RS row: bind off remaining 3 (4, 5, 7, 9) sts.

SLEEVES
With smaller needles, cast on 48 (48, 52, 54, 62) sts. Work in k1, p1 rib for 12 rows.
Change to larger needles and work 6 rows even in stockinette st.
Work increases 2 sts in from edge as follows: K2, LLI, knit to last 3 sts, RLI, k2. Continue to increase every 8 rows on the RS 16 (17, 17, 17, 19) more times; 82 (84, 88, 90, 102) sts.
Work even until sleeve measures 17 (17, 17 ½, 18, 18)" or desired length to underarm.

Shape sleeve cap
Bind off 4 (4, 6, 6, 7) sts at beginning of next 2 rows; 74 (76, 76, 78, 88) sts.
Begin decreasing 2 sts in from edge every other row on RS as follows: K2, k2tog, knit to last 4 sts, ssk, k2 sts 19 (17, 14, 19, 25) times; 36 (42, 48, 40, 38) sts.
Begin decreasing every 4 rows on the RS: K2, k2tog,

knit to last 4 sts, ssk, k2 sts 5 (8, 10, 8, 6) times; 26 (26, 28, 24, 26) sts.
Bind off 3 (3, 3, 2, 2) sts at beginning of next 4 rows; 14 (14, 16, 16, 18) sts.
Bind off remaining sts.

FINISHING
Sew fronts to back at shoulder seams. Sew in sleeve caps. Sew side and underarm seams.

Buttonband
Using smaller needles and with RS facing, beginning at neck edge, pick up and k116 (125, 129, 131, 135) sts along left front. Work in k1, p1 rib for 7 rows. Bind off using the k2tbl loop method (see appendix).
Place 8 split ring markers or coilless pins for buttons as follows: place button ¼" from lower edge; place button at the top of button band and space other buttons evenly in between.

Buttonhole band
Work as for left front, but make small buttonholes in second row (yo, ssk) to correspond to each marker. Finish as for left front.

Neck band
With smaller needles, pick up and k46 (46, 50, 50, 54) sts along right front neckline, pick up and k45 (47, 51, 51, 55)

sts across back, then 46 (46, 50, 50, 54) sts along left front neckline; 137 (139, 151, 151, 163) sts. Work in k1, p1 rib for 1 row. In next row, place buttonhole: k1, p1, k1, k2tog, yo, finish row in rib. Work k1, p1 rib for 5 more rows. Bind off using k2tbl loop bind-off method.

Sew on buttons. Weave in ends. Block garment.

VARIATIONS
Mitered band Euroflax and Pediboo versions
Note: For contrast hem version begin with CC (charcoal), change to MC (lilac) on RS row 8.

BACK
With larger needles, cast on 104 (118, 126, 134, 146) sts. Change to smaller needles and work in stockinette st for 9 rows. This forms the hem facing.

Turning row: On next WS row, knit.
Change to larger needles and beginning with a RS row, work in stockinette st for 7 rows.
Fold hem facing along fold line so wrong sides are together. Knit each st on the needle together with the corresponding st of the cast-on row. Work 4 rows in stockinette st.
Continue as for Kidsilk Haze sweater, beginning at waist shaping.

RIGHT FRONT
With larger needles, cast on 50 (57, 61, 65, 71) sts. Change to smaller needles and work in stockinette st for 9 rows. This forms the hem facing.
Turning row: On next WS row, knit.
Change to larger needles and beginning with next RS row, work in stockinette st for 7 rows.

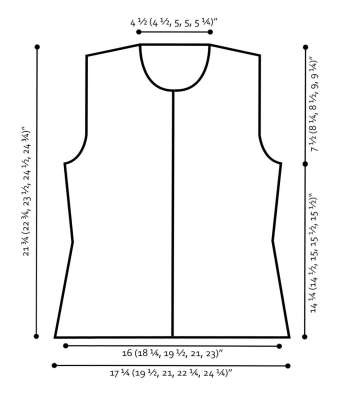

4 ½ (4 ½, 5, 5, 5 ¼)"

7 ½ (8 ¼, 8 ½, 9, 9 ¼)"

21 ¾ (22 ¾, 23 ½, 24 ½, 24 ¾)"

14 ¼ (14 ½, 15, 15 ½, 15 ½)"

16 (18 ¼, 19 ½, 21, 23)"

17 ¼ (19 ½, 21, 22 ¼, 24 ¼)"

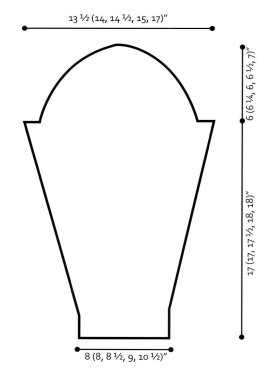

13 ½ (14, 14 ½, 15, 17)"

6 (6 ¼, 6, 6 ½, 7)"

17 (17, 17 ½, 18, 18)"

8 (8, 8 ½, 9, 10 ½)"

Join hem as for back. Work 4 rows in stockinette st. Continue as for right front of Kidsilk Haze sweater, beginning at waist shaping.

LEFT FRONT

Work as for right front for hem. Work 4 rows in stockinette st. Continue as for left front of Kidsilk Haze sweater.

SLEEVE

With larger needles, cast on 48 (48, 52, 54, 62) sts. Change to smaller needles and work in stockinette st for 9 rows. This forms the hem facing.

Turning row: On next WS row, knit.

Change to larger needles and beginning with next RS row, work in stockinette st for 7 rows.

Fold hem facing along fold line so wrong sides are together. Knit each st on the needle together with the corresponding st of the cast-on row. Work 8 rows in stockinette st.

Continue as for sleeves of Kidsilk Haze sweater, beginning with increases after ribbing.

Mitered facing border

With larger needles and beginning at lower right-hand corner of front, pick up and k104 (110, 114, 118, 122) sts. At right front neck edge, M1, pick up and k1 st, place a pin or split ring marker in st, M1. Pick up and k30 (30, 32, 34, 36) sts across right front neck edge, M1, pick up and k1 st, place pin or marker in st, M1. Pick up and k40 (40, 42, 44, 46) sts across neck back. M1, pick up and k1 st, place pin or marker in st, M1. Pick up and k30 (30, 32, 34, 36) sts on right front. M1, pick up and k1 st, place pin or marker in st, M1. Pick up and k104 (110, 114, 118, 122) sts along left front.

Purl 1 row.

On next row: Knit to marked st, M1, knit marked st, M1, knit to next marked st, M1, knit marked st M1, knit to end. Continue in stockinette st, repeating the increase every RS row 4 times (8 rows total).

Turning row: On next WS row, knit.

Change to smaller needles and on next RS row, knit to 2 sts before marked st, ssk, k1, k2tog, knit to 2 sts before next marked st, ssk, k1, k2tog, knit to end. Work the same number of rows as the front (not counting turning row). Bind off loosely with k2tbl bind-off method *(see appendix)*. Fold border; sew in place.

man's sweater
by Mary Lou Egan

Size
Man's small (medium, large, x-large, xx-large)
Finished chest circumference: 38 (42, 46, 50, 54)", zipped

Materials
Ultra Alpaca from Berroco (215 yards per 100-gram skein):
  6 (6, 7, 7, 8) skeins of color A (Charcoal mix #6289) and
  1 skein each of colors B (Carrots orange #6263) and
  C (Winter white #6201)

Knitting needles size US 4 (3.5 mm) and size US 7 (4.5 mm)
  and/or 32-inch or 40-inch circular knitting needles size
  US 4 and size US 7 for front band or size needed to obtain
  gauge
Blunt tapestry needle
4 stitch holders
Split ring stitch marker
Separating zipper, 22 (22, 22, 24, 24)" long, or custom length
  cut to fit
Crochet hook size F
Straight pins
Sewing needle and matching thread

Gauge
In stockinette st with larger needles, 20 sts and 28 rows = 4"

TO KNIT
BACK
With color A (charcoal) and smaller needles, cast on 96 (106, 116, 126, 136) sts. Work in k1, p1 rib for 13 rows. Change to larger needles and work in stockinette st (k1 row, p1 row) until piece measures 16" from cast-on edge or desired length to underarm, ending with a WS row.

Shape armholes
Bind off 5 sts at the beginning of the next 2 rows. On next row, decrease 1 st at each end as follows: K1, ssk, knit to end, k2tog, k1. Continue to decrease in this manner every other row 2 more times; 80 (90, 100, 110, 120) sts.
Work until back measures 25 ½ (25 ¾, 26 ¼, 26 ½, 27)" from cast-on edge, ending with a WS row.
K25 (28, 32, 35, 38) sts for shoulder; bind off center 30 (34, 36, 40, 44) sts for back neck, k25 (28, 32, 35, 38) sts for second shoulder. Place shoulder sts on holders.

RIGHT FRONT (as worn)
With color A and smaller needles, cast on 44 (49, 54, 59, 64) sts. Work in k1, p1 rib for 13 rows. Change to larger needles and work in stockinette st until piece measures same as back to underarm, ending with a RS row.

Shape armholes
Bind off 5 sts at the beginning of the next WS row. Decrease 1 st at end of next RS row as follows: knit to last 3 sts, k2tog, k1. Continue to decrease every other row 2 more times; 36 (41, 46, 51, 56) sts.

Work until front measures 22 ½ (22 ¾, 23 ¼, 23 ½, 24)" from cast-on edge, ending with a WS row.

Shape front neck
At beginning of next 2 RS rows, bind off 3 sts. Purl 1 row.
Bind off 2 sts at neck edge on next RS row, then every other row 0 (1, 2, 3, 4) more times. Purl 1 row.
Bind off 1 st at neck edge on next RS row, then every 4 rows 2 (2, 1, 1, 1) times. You have decreased 11 (13, 14, 16, 18) sts; 25 (28, 32, 35, 38) sts remain for shoulder.
Work even until front measures same as back to shoulder; place sts on holder for shoulder.

LEFT FRONT
With color A and smaller needles, cast on 44 (49, 54, 59, 64) sts. Work in k1, p1 rib for 13 rows. Change to larger needles and work in stockinette st until piece measures same as back to underarm, ending with a WS row.

Shape armhole
Bind off 5 sts at the beginning of next RS row. Purl 1 row.
Decrease 1 st at beginning of next RS row as follows: K1, ssk, knit remaining sts. Continue to decrease every other row 2 more times; 36 (41, 46, 51, 56) sts.
Work until left front measures same as right front to neck shaping, ending with a RS row.

Shape front neck
At beginning of next 2 WS rows, bind off 3 sts. Knit 1 row.
Bind off 2 sts at neck edge on next WS row, then every other row 0 (1, 2, 3, 4) times. Knit 1 row.
Bind off 1 st at neck edge on next WS row, then every 4 rows 2 (2, 1, 1, 1) more times; you have decreased 11 (13, 14, 16, 18) sts; 25 (28, 32, 35, 38) sts remain for shoulder.
Work even until front measures same as back to shoulder; place sts on holder for shoulder.

SLEEVES
With color A and smaller needles, cast on 44 (44, 46, 48, 50) sts. Work in k1, p1 rib for 13 rows. Change to larger needles and work 4 rows even in stockinette st.
Work increases at each end of next RS row as follows: k1, M1, knit to last st, M1, k1. Then increase every 4 rows 17 (23, 22, 22, 25) more times, then every 6 rows 8 (4, 6, 6, 4) more times; 96 (100, 104, 106, 110) sts.
Work even until sleeve measures 19 ½ (19 ½, 20 ½, 20 ½, 20 ½)" or desired length.

Shape sleeve cap
Decrease 1 st at each end as follows: k1, ssk, knit to last 3 sts, k2tog, k1. Then decrease every other row 3 more times; 88 (92, 96, 98, 102) sts. Bind off all sts.
Repeat for second sleeve.

FINISHING
Join front and back at shoulders using three-needle bind off (see appendix).
Sew in sleeves, matching angles at armhole. Sew side and underarm seams.

Neck band
With color A and larger needles, pick up and k24 sts along right front neck, 30 (34, 36, 40, 44) sts across back, 24 sts along left front neck; 78 (82, 84, 88, 92) sts total.
Work 13 rows in stockinette st. Knit 2 rows (to create turning row).

Change to color B (orange) and smaller needles, knit 14 rows in stockinette st. Bind off loosely.

Front band
With color A and larger needles, pick up and knit approximately 108 (110, 112, 114, 116) sts along front edge. *Note:* If you lengthened or shortened the sweater, you will pick up a different number of sts. Pick up about 2 out of every 3 sts. Knit 1 row (for purl ridge on RS).
Change to color C (white) and work 5 rows stockinette st.
Change to color A and knit 2 rows (to create turning row), Purl 1 row. Work 4 more rows in stockinette st. Bind off.
Repeat for other front band.

Vertical chain detail

On right front, mark the column of stitches 2 sts in from front band. With color B (orange) and size F crochet hook, pick up approximately 2 out of every 3 sts and crochet as follows: with yarn held to back, beginning at bottom, hold onto tail of yarn, push hook through stitch from front to back, yarn over, pull loop through to front. Move to next st up, insert hook, and pull yarn through loop on hook. Continue in this manner to top of collar. Repeat for left front.

Fold neck and front bands and sew in place. Weave in ends. Block garment.

Zipper

Pin zipper in place with straight pins or baste with long running stitches. Try on sweater and adjust placement of zipper if necessary. Sew zipper in place.

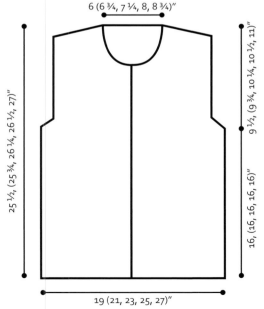

6 (6 ¾, 7 ¼, 8, 8 ¾)"

9 ½, (9 ¾, 10 ¼, 10 ½, 11)"

25 ½, (25 ¾, 26 ¼, 26 ½, 27)"

16, (16, 16, 16, 16)"

19 (21, 23, 25, 27)"

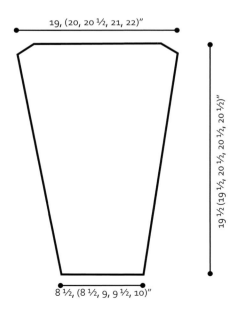

19, (20, 20 ½, 21, 22)"

19 ½ (19 ½, 20 ½, 20 ½, 20 ½)"

8 ½, (8 ½, 9, 9 ½, 10)"

table runner

by Peggy Lexau

Size

Finished measurements: 14" wide by 57" long

Materials

Euroflax Linen sport-weight yarn from Louet (270 yards per 100-gram skein): 2 skeins color A (Natural #36) and 1 skein each color B (Eggplant #42) and color C (Cream #30).

40-inch circular knitting needles size US 5 (3.75mm) or size needed to obtain gauge
Tapestry needle

Gauge

In stockinette st, 22 sts and 34 rows = 4" before blocking; 20 sts and 32 rows = 4" after blocking

Seed stitch pattern

Worked over an even number of sts.
Row 1: *K1, p1; repeat from * across.
Row 2: *P1, k1; repeat from * across.
Repeat rows 1-2 for pattern.

TO KNIT

Note: Bottom, top, and side borders will all be worked in seed st. On several rows of the pattern, you will slide all sts to the other end of the needle to work the next row, rather than turning your work. On these rows, you change the sequence of knit and purl sts to keep the seed st edges correct.

With color A (natural), cast on 288 sts.

Beginning border

Rows 1-4: Work in seed st.
Row 5 (WS): Work in seed st for first 4 sts; purl to the last 4 sts; work last 4 sts in seed st.
Row 6 (RS): Keeping first and last 4 sts in seed st, knit across row.
Rows 7-11: Keeping first and last 4 sts in seed st, continue working in stockinette st.

Wide stripe section

Stripe 1
Row 12 (RS): Join color B (eggplant), seed st 4, *k1, sl 1 wyif; rep from * to last 4 sts; seed st 4.
Row 13 (WS): With color B, seed st 4, purl to last 4 sts, seed st 4.
Row 14 (RS): With color A, seed st 4, k2, sl 1 wyif, *k1, sl 1 wyif; rep from * to last 6 sts; k2, seed st 4. Cut color A at the end of this row; leave 5" tail to weave in later.
Row 15 (RS): *Do not turn work.* Slide sts to other end of

needle where color B yarn is available. With color B, seed st 4, knit to last 4 sts, seed st 4.

Rows 16-20: With color B and keeping edges in seed st, work in stockinette st.

Stripe 2

Row 21 (RS): Join color C (cream), seed st 4, *k1, sl 1 wyif; rep from * to last 4 sts; seed st 4.

Row 22 (WS): With color C, seed st 4, purl to last 4 sts, seed st 4.

Row 23 (RS): With color B, seed st 4, k2, sl 1 wyif, *k1, sl 1 wyif; rep from * to last 6 sts; k2, seed st 4.

Row 24 (WS): With color B, seed st 4, purl to last 4 sts, seed st 4.

Stripe 3

Row 25 (RS): With color C, seed st 4, *k1, sl 1 wyif; rep from * to last 6 sts; k2, seed st 4. Cut color C, leaving tail to weave in later.

Row 26 (RS): *Do not turn work.* Slide sts to other end of needle where color B yarn is available. With color B, seed st 4, knit across to last 4 sts, seed st 4.

Rows 27-31: With color B and keeping edges in seed st, work in stockinette st.

Row 32 (RS): Join color A, seed st 4, *k1, sl 1 wyif; rep from * to last 4 sts, seed st 4.

Row 33 (WS): With color A, seed st 4, purl across to last 4 sts, seed st 4.

Row 34 (RS): With color B, seed st 4, k2, sl 1 wyif, *k1, sl 1 wyif; rep from * to last 6 sts, k2, seed st 4. Cut color B, leaving tail to weave in later.

Row 35 (RS): *Do not turn work.* Slide sts to other end of needle where color A yarn is available. With color A, seed st 4, knit to last 4 sts, seed st 4.

Separator stripe

Rows 36-38: With color A and keeping edges in seed st, work in stockinette st.

Narrow stripe section

Stripe 1

Row 39 (RS): Join color B, seed st 4, *k1, sl 1 wyif; rep from

* to last 4 sts, seed st 4.

Rows 40-42: With color B and keeping edges in seed st, work in stockinette st.

Stripe 2

Row 43 (RS): With color C, seed st 4, *k1, sl 1 wyif; rep from * to last 4 sts, seed st 4.

Row 44 (WS): With color C, seed st 4, purl to last 4 sts, seed st 4. Cut color C, leaving tail to weave in later.

Stripe 3

Row 45 (RS): With color B, k2, sl 1 wyif, *k1, sl 1 wyif; rep from * to last 6 sts, k2, seed st 4.

Rows 46-48: With color B and keeping edges in seed st, work in stockinette st.

Row 49 (RS): With color A, seed st 4, *k1, sl 1wyif; rep from * to last 4 sts, seed st 4.

Center section

Rows 50-80: With color A and keeping edges in seed st, work in stockinette st.

Narrow stripe section

Rows 81-91: Repeat rows 39-49.

Separator stripe

Rows 92-94: Repeat rows 36-38.

Wide stripe section

Rows 95-118: Repeat rows 12-35.

Ending border

Rows 119-125: Continuing with color A and keeping edges in seed st, work in stockinette st.

Rows 126-129: With color A, work in seed stitch. Bind off all sts knitwise.

FINISHING

Weave in ends. Wash and dry flat to block, pinning to dimensions as desired. Over time, the linen will become softer; the dimensions may change slightly with multiple washings.

appendix

ABBREVIATIONS

CC: contrast color
CO: cast on
dec: decrease
inc: increase
LLI (Left lifted increase): With left needle, lift left leg of stitch below last knitted stitch onto needle and knit this stitch.
K or k: knit
kfb: knit in front and back (increasing 1 stitch)
k2tog: knit 2 stitches together
k2tog tbl: Knit 2 stitches together through back loops
kw: knitwise; slip stitch as if to knit.
m: marker
MC: main color
M1 (make 1): Make a loop cast-on onto right-hand needle to increase 1 stitch.
pm: place marker
P or p: purl
rep: repeat
RLI (Right lifted increase): With right needle, lift first leg of stitch below the next stitch onto left needle and knit this stitch.
RS: right side
sl: slip
sl m: slip marker
sl1-k2tog-psso: slip 1 stitch, knit next 2 stitches together, pass slipped stitch over
sl 1 wyif: slip a stitch as if to purl with yarn in front
ssk (slip, slip, knit): Slip next 2 stitches to right-hand needle one at a time as if to knit. Insert left-hand needle into front loops of stitches just slipped. Wrap yarn and draw through. You have just decreased 1 stitch.
stockinette st: knit 1 row (right side); purl 1 row (wrong side)
st(s): stitch(es)
wyif: with yarn in front
wyib: with yarn in back
WS: wrong side
yo: yarnover

TECHNIQUES

k2tbl bind off: *Knit 2 stitches together through the back loop. Return the stitch back to the left-hand needle; repeat from *.

Kitchener stitch: Thread a blunt tapestry needle with the tail of yarn. Holding the two knitting needles parallel:

Step 1: Insert tapestry needle into first stitch of front needle as if to knit and slip the stitch off.

Step 2: Insert tapestry needle into second stitch of front needle as if to purl, leaving the stitch on the knitting needle, draw the yarn through.

Step 3: Insert tapestry needle into first stitch of back needle as if to purl and slip the stitch off.

Step 4: Insert tapestry needle into second stitch of back needle as if to knit, leaving the stitch on the knitting needle, draw the yarn through.

Repeat these 4 steps until all stitches are woven together.

Mattress stitch: Technique for sewing invisible seams. Visit wearwithallbook.com for illustration.

Three-needle bind-off: Place shoulder stitches from holders onto 2 separate needles with right sides facing. Using third needle, insert knitwise into the first stitch of each needle, wrap as for a knit stitch and draw yarn through both stitches. You will have one stitch on right-hand needle.

Do the same for the next stitch on each needle. You have 2 stitches on the right-hand needle. Now, bind off the first stitch you made over the second stitch. Knit the next stitch from each needle and continue to bind off.

acknowledgments

We are grateful for the generosity and vision of Marge Maddux, Peter and Linda Kreisman, James and Marion Seeley Kreisman, owners of The Yarnery, Saint Paul, Minnesota. The Yarnery has been a Saint Paul institution for 40 years, and a destination for all those who love to knit, crochet, and weave. The Kreisman family remains dedicated to innovation, quality, and above all, a love of excellent yarn.

Extraordinary test knitters all, you improved every design with your meticulous work: Linda Kreisman Marge Maddux, Martha Alvarado, Sherry Enzler, Barbara Moon, Susan Kolstad-Onken, Angela Paulson, Melissa Rogan, Calvin McManamy, Susan Seltz, Carol Stumme, Breanne Nelson, Iris Blackketter, Rita Schmitt, Ellen Silva, Tetsuya Shimano, Lynn Collins McElin.

We are inspired every day by your yarn, and thrilled to feature it in these pages: Warren Wheelock, Berroco (berroco.com); Tricia and Chet Petkiewicz, Frog Tree Yarns (frogtreeyarns.com); Jean Dunbabin, Cascade Yarns (cascadeyarns.com); Kim Lui and David Codling, TUTTO Opal-Isager (knitisager.com); Nancy Kleiber and Jessica Lacasse, Rowan/Westminster Fibers (westminsterfibers.com); David Van Stralen, Louet (louet.com).

Models, you wore the clothes well, and were cooperative, fun, and easy-going throughout an exhausting photo shoot: Ali Jacobsen, Adam Carter, Malika Sadi-Goodman, Voyta Meyer , Maya Alvarado, Leo Lunder, Kai Nelson, Danny Rogan, Juniper Geffner, Asher Kempe.

Malika Sadi-Goodman, we are quite sure there is no better stylist anywhere. You anticipated every need, made impeccable choices, and improved every photo with your painstaking work.

Everyone at the photo shoot coveted the jewelry crafted by Hans Early-Nelson (precisionmetalcraft.com) and Liz Parent (madebylizp.com).

Thank you Greg Martin, Urban Bean Coffee, Lyndale Avenue, Minneapolis (urbanbeancoffee.com)—you provided a great location for a photo shoot, and make an even better cup of coffee.

Brian Nordin, Bann Business Solutions (bannbiz.com), you made publishing a book seem, if not easy, then at least manageable, with your friendly, pragmatic advice.

Family and friends, we are most grateful for your support, for listening to our never-ending talk of yarn and knitting, and for encouraging us at every turn.

(l to r): Mary Lou Egan, Scott Rohr, Theresa Gaffey, Sarah K. Walker, Shelly Sheehan

All the yarn referenced in *Wearwithall* can be ordered at yarnery.com. Visit The Yarnery's website to find more information about the full range of yarns offered, as well as classes, events, hours and directions. We would love for you to visit, and of course, we'll sign your copy of *Wearwithall*!